POSITIVE AFFIRMATIONS AND ACTIONS FOR
Gratitude

PRACTICE POSITIVITY, HAPPINESS
AND MINDFULNESS WITH DAILY
RITUALS OF THANKFULNESS

🐢 Turtle Publishing

Published by Turtle Publishing
All rights reserved.

Printed on demand in Australia, United States and United Kingdom.

Written & designed by Kathy Shanks
© Kathy Shanks 2021
Illustrations by Freepik Storyset & Turtle Publishing

No part of this publication may be reproduced, stored in a retrieval system, or transmitted in any form or by any means, electronic, mechanical, photocopying, recording or otherwise, without the prior written permission of the author.

Under no circumstances will any blame or legal responsibility be held against the publisher, or author, for any damages, reparation, or monetary loss due to the information contained within this book including, but not limited to — errors, omissions, or inaccuracies. Either directly or indirectly. You are responsible for your own choices, actions, and results.

Legal Notice: This book is copyright protected. This book is only for personal use. You cannot amend, distribute, sell, use, quote or paraphrase any part, or the content within this book, without the consent of the author or publisher.

Disclaimer: Please note the information contained within this document is for educational and entertainment purposes only. All effort has been executed to present accurate, up to date, and reliable, complete information. No warranties of any kind are declared or implied. Readers acknowledge that the author is not engaging in the rendering of legal, financial, medical or professional advice. The content within this book has been derived from various sources. Please consult a licensed professional before attempting any techniques outlined in this book.

SPECIAL BONUS
FREE BOOKS

FREE Workbook to begin an intentional journaling practice.

FREE 30 Days to Greater Self Love Program

Get FREE unlimited access to these AND all of my new books by joining our fan base!

SCAN WITH YOUR CAMERA OR GO TO
bit.ly/AffGifts

How to use this book

On the left-hand pages are affirmations. On the right-hand pages are actions for you to take towards strengthening your gratitude.

You may like to work through this book one page per day, or perhaps you'd like to trust divine guidance. Hold this book close to your heart or navel, close your eyes, take three gentle breaths, and as you breathe out on the third breath, open the book. We trust that you will be guided to the page you need the most.

Introduction

Imagine your typical day.

You wake up bright and early and go about your morning rituals. Perhaps you kick off the day by whipping up some breakfast for yourself or your family before diving into everything else on your 'to-do' list. Most likely, the rest of the day is spent on things you *need* to do—maybe going to work, or taking care of the kids and making sure your household is in order, as well as running various seemingly never-ending errands. If you have a bit more time, maybe you're able to squeeze in the things you *want* to do—meeting up with friends, working on a hobby or personal project, or maybe getting in a quick workout.

No matter what your day looks like, chances are, you get by with a little help—from friends, family, and members of the community around you, the privileges and conveniences you enjoy, or even a greater force at work, be it nature, the universe, or any spiritual power.

Take that typical day, for example. The food on the table fuels you for the rest of your activities. The love from your significant other or your kids nourishes you, too, giving you a boost of motivation to carry with you. You might have teammates you collaborate with at work to produce amazing output. Even while out and about, say, at the supermarket or service centre, you encounter people who are ready to assist you in one way or another. Not to mention the *things* at your disposal—a car or public transport to get you where you need to go, your mobile to keep you connected, a place to call home.

There are *so many* people, things, and circumstances that support us and make each day possible. But, as we go about our daily lives, how often do we stop and express thanks? How much energy do we send towards gratitude?

It's all too easy to get caught up in both the hustle of our daily lives, as well as keeping sight of our long-term vision and goals. We rush from one thing to the next, barely having enough time for everything that has to get done, much less to take a step back and give thanks.

There's no denying that life can be *tough*, too. The difficulties, setbacks, and obstacles that are all an inevitable part of life can loom unfortunately large, blocking your view of the things that are going *right*—of everything else to be grateful for.

Despite these challenges, though, cultivating gratitude is incredibly important in living a full life. The truth is, it can be downright life-changing.

Nurturing a grateful heart allows contentment into your life. Instead of taking note of all that's lacking or that you still want, gratitude enables you to refocus on what you *already have*. It helps you get unstuck from 'what can be' and grounds you in 'what is.' You might be surprised at how happy you could be *right this moment*, just by recognising everything you have for what it truly is.

Not only does practising gratitude do wonders for you mentally and emotionally, but it actually impacts your physical health as well. Simply put, our thoughts, feelings, and actions engage different parts of the brain—pain activates a specific area, excitement taps another, and so on. Being grateful and recognising others' positive actions are processed in a region that's associated with socialisation and pleasure. Both of these are, in turn, connected to other parts of the brain that are responsible for stress relief and physical relaxation.

Gratitude is also extremely important in forming relationships and strengthening bonds with other people. Without even expressing thanks, *simply being* grateful involves recognising the positive impact others have on our lives and the ties that connect us with one another. Affirming *others* and the positive impact they have on your life galvanises your experience of being grateful. In expressing your sincere appreciation verbally or through any other means, you kindle the fire of gratitude within, keeping it burning brighter than ever. At its very core, gratitude pushes us to see the good in others.

In working towards more gratitude in your life, remember that it is a *practice*. Gratitude is more than a passive emotion—in fact, you probably subconsciously have that part of it covered already. After all, weren't we all brought up with good manners that include habitual, automatic 'thank you's?' Aren't we constantly taught to count our blessings?

True gratitude goes beyond that, though. It is a state of mindfulness combined with intentional action.

In exploring and cultivating a deeper sense of gratitude, an affirmation practice can allow you to pause and re-centre, focusing on the positivity in your life. It can be a powerful tool for identifying and really acknowledging each specific thing that you are grateful for.

"I am happy because I'm grateful. I choose to be grateful. That gratitude allows me to be happy."

- Will Arnett

AFFIRMATIONS

With each day, the gratitude in my heart only grows.

ACTIONS

Before you go to bed, make a list of 5 good things that happened or that you experienced throughout the day.

AFFIRMATIONS

I draw
happiness from
giving thanks.

ACTIONS

Write a 'thank you' note to 3 people who have touched your life.

AFFIRMATIONS

I am overjoyed
to be alive.

ACTIONS

Begin each day with gratitude. Even before getting up and out of bed, give thanks for the new day.

AFFIRMATIONS

I am grateful for my space in this world and the universe.

ACTIONS

Practice being mindful and intentional each time you say 'thank you' to someone.
Even for little everyday things, try to really let the gratitude wash over you as you say it.

AFFIRMATIONS

Recognising and giving thanks for everything I have is a part of who I am.

ACTIONS

Go on a walk outdoors and take notice of all the wonderful things you encounter along the way— the sights, sounds, sensations, and everything in between.

AFFIRMATIONS

I am thankful for what I already have, and everything that I know is yet to come.

ACTIONS

Write a 'thank you' letter to your past self—remember, you wouldn't be who you are today if not for them.

AFFIRMATIONS

I am grateful for my body and everything it allows me to do.

ACTIONS

Reflect on your journey so far. How has your life changed for the better in the past 5 years?

AFFIRMATIONS

I can always find something to be grateful for, no matter how small.

ACTIONS

Spend quality time with your loved ones, just enjoying each other's company and being together.

AFFIRMATIONS

I honour and appreciate all the amazing people in my life.

ACTIONS

Reach out to thank someone you have learned something from.

AFFIRMATIONS

Gratitude holds tremendous power in my life.

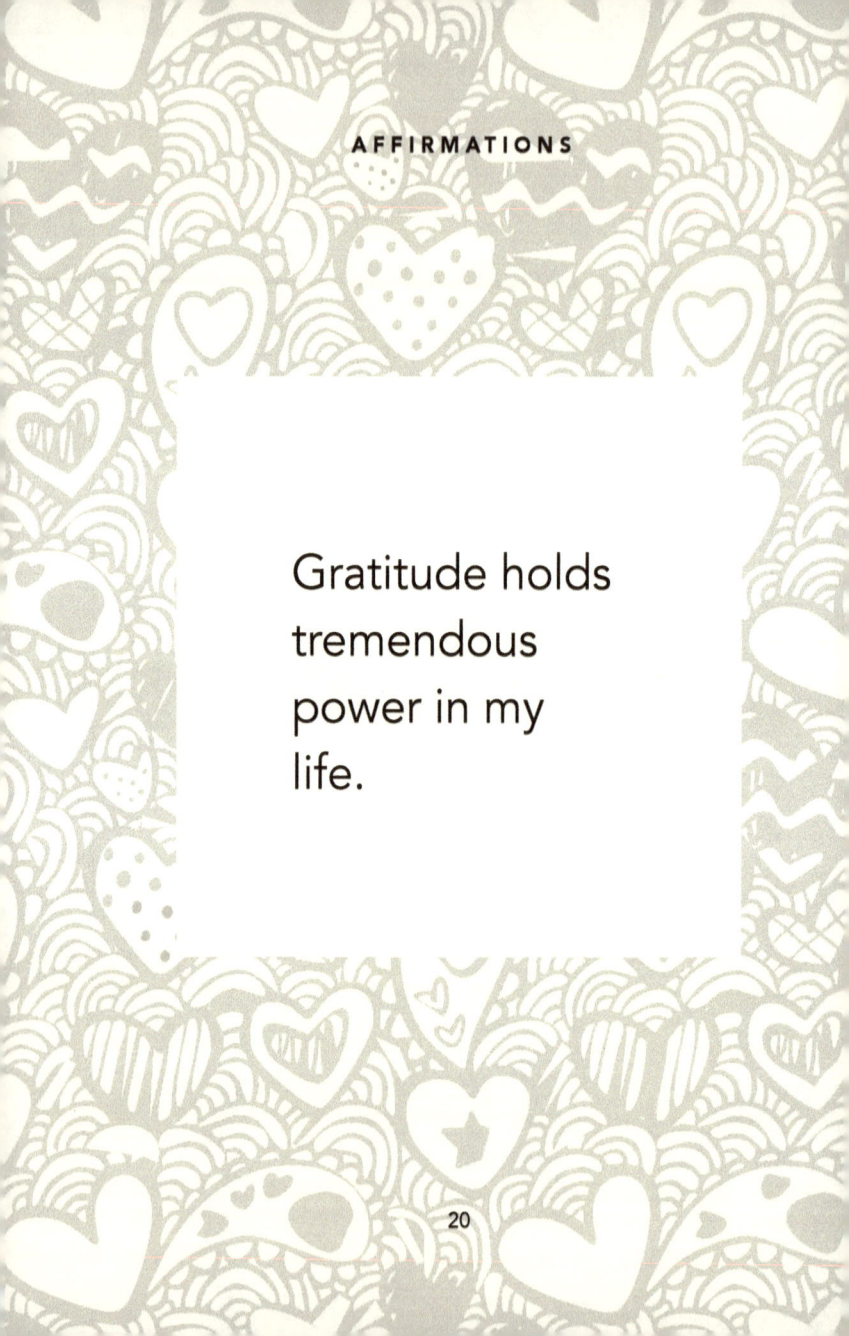

ACTIONS

Giving is gratitude in action. Do something nice for someone else as a way of 'paying it forward.'

AFFIRMATIONS

My gratitude fuels and inspires me.

ACTIONS

Prepare a small token of appreciation for a service worker who regularly makes your life a little better.

AFFIRMATIONS

I am filled with gratitude for my journey so far, as well as the journey ahead.

ACTIONS

Make a loved one their favourite meal.

AFFIRMATIONS

I give thanks for the challenges that have shaped who I am.

ACTIONS

Designate one day a week as your 'no complaints' day.

AFFIRMATIONS

My life is made infinitely richer by giving thanks for everything I have.

ACTIONS

Set up a visual reminder of gratitude—a simple family memento or favourite snapshot will usually do the trick.

AFFIRMATIONS

My grateful heart is beautiful.

ACTIONS

When faced with an obstacle or difficult situation, pause to ask yourself, "What can I learn from this?"

AFFIRMATIONS

I am grateful for today.

ACTIONS

Share something you love—maybe a favourite song or book, or even just a recently discovered life hack—with a friend.

AFFIRMATIONS

Gratitude flows easily through all the areas of my life.

ACTIONS

Set a timer for 60 seconds, and list down as many positive things in your life as you can in that minute.

AFFIRMATIONS

My mind is filled with appreciation for the world around me.

ACTIONS

Accept others' gratitude openly. Allow yourself to truly feel it when someone thanks you.

AFFIRMATIONS

I am grateful for every breath that fills my lungs.

ACTIONS

Set aside some time each day to simply be present and reflect on the things you are grateful for.

AFFIRMATIONS

I love the life
that I lead.

ACTIONS

Send someone a song that reminds you of them.

AFFIRMATIONS

I am grateful to have the opportunity to impact others' lives positively.

ACTIONS

Think back to something that made you laugh out loud (or at least crack a really big smile) recently.

AFFIRMATIONS

I live each day in awe of the universe.

ACTIONS

Write a letter to your personal hero. You can keep it to yourself or go ahead and send it to them—it's totally up to you.

AFFIRMATIONS

Every day brings new chances to be grateful.

ACTIONS

Listen to a song that brings you back to one of your favourite moments ever.

AFFIRMATIONS

I begin and end each day with gratitude.

ACTIONS

Write down the 3 biggest lessons you are grateful to have learned so far in life.

AFFIRMATIONS

I approach life with a sense of wonder.

ACTIONS

Have you recently purchased from a small business or tried a local restaurant? Write a glowing review of something you enjoyed.

AFFIRMATIONS

I never take anything for granted.

ACTIONS

What are you excited about? Write down what you are looking forward to in the next week, month, and year.

AFFIRMATIONS

I find huge joy in even the smallest of things.

ACTIONS

Write about your favourite memory with your best friend and share it with them.

AFFIRMATIONS

I am perfectly content with where I am in life.

ACTIONS

Tell your friends and family you love them whenever you feel it—say it out loud and without hesitation.

AFFIRMATIONS

I recognise all the privileges that I am blessed with.

ACTIONS

Set aside a few minutes to practice or exercise a skill you're grateful to have.

AFFIRMATIONS

I am grateful to be able to pursue my passions in life.

ACTIONS

Write a letter of gratitude for your hopes for your future. Use gratitude to manifest your dreams.

AFFIRMATIONS

I am beyond thankful for my family, friends, and loved ones.

ACTIONS

After attending events like birthday celebrations or dinner parties, make it a habit to send handwritten notes of appreciation to the hosts.

AFFIRMATIONS

With every breath, I give thanks.

ACTIONS

Make time to cuddle with your partner, kids, pets… anyone you're grateful to love and be loved by.

AFFIRMATIONS

I focus on the good and let go of the bad.

ACTIONS

Organise your favourite photos into albums or maybe even a creative collage you can frame and hang up on the wall.

AFFIRMATIONS

I turn my gratitude into action.

ACTIONS

Show appreciation for a friend or relative by putting together a personalised care package for them.

AFFIRMATIONS

My life is filled with things to be grateful for.

ACTIONS

Write about the last time you felt completely content and happy.

AFFIRMATIONS

I find peace in gratitude.

ACTIONS

Go somewhere you can really immerse in nature—the beach or mountains are always a great idea. While you're there, take a moment to reflect on how it feels to be part of this great big world.

AFFIRMATIONS

I am grateful for
the room I still
have for growth.

ACTIONS

Take someone on a tour of all your favourite spots in your neighbourhood.

AFFIRMATIONS

My existence is meaningful and purposeful.

ACTIONS

Do you have a mentor, coach, or teacher who has made a profound impact on your life? Reach out to them and let them know how much you appreciate them.

AFFIRMATIONS

I trust what life has in store for me.

ACTIONS

Even just for a day, take over the chores usually done by someone else in your household.

AFFIRMATIONS

I am grateful for my talents, skills, and abilities.

ACTIONS

Tip generously whenever you enjoy exceptional service at a restaurant.

AFFIRMATIONS

The universe
favours me and
supports me.

ACTIONS

At work, publicly thank and maybe even officially acknowledge someone who helped you out with something or contributed to your team's efforts.

AFFIRMATIONS

I am grateful for every person who has touched my life in some way, whether big or small.

ACTIONS

Come up with a list of 5 positive things in your life that you might be taking for granted—dig deep. How do these make your life better? How can you be more mindfully appreciative of these moving forward?

AFFIRMATIONS

Gratitude
comes naturally
to me.

ACTIONS

Think of your least favourite part of the day or week. Now, try to find something positive about it.

AFFIRMATIONS

I am proud of
my grateful
heart and mind.

ACTIONS

Show your body appreciation for everything it does for you by fuelling up with a meal that's both delicious and healthy.

AFFIRMATIONS

Gratitude uplifts me and sets me up for success.

ACTIONS

Write about something you have worked hard for and that you are grateful to have finally gotten or achieved.

AFFIRMATIONS

I allow gratitude to transform my soul for the better.

ACTIONS

Get a deeper appreciation for the food you enjoy by taking a 'field trip' to your local farm.

AFFIRMATIONS

Gratitude opens doors for great things to come into my life.

ACTIONS

What's a memorable tradition you appreciated growing up? How can you bring this back now in your adult life?

AFFIRMATIONS

I am grateful for all the things I am given a chance to experience in this life—good, bad, and everything in between.

ACTIONS

Think of someone you love, and list down 10 of your favourite things about them.

AFFIRMATIONS

I accept challenges with a grateful heart, as these are opportunities to grow.

ACTIONS

Put on your favourite song, and jot down a description of how it makes you feel.

AFFIRMATIONS

The positive energy of gratitude radiates deep within my soul.

ACTIONS

Write about the biggest obstacle you've overcome in your life.

AFFIRMATIONS

I invite the seeds of gratitude to take root in my soul.

ACTIONS

Experience something—go somewhere you've never been before, try a new activity—for the first time.

AFFIRMATIONS

I am thankful for the material possessions I have.

ACTIONS

Reflect on why gratitude is important to you. You could meditate on it, write down your thoughts, or talk it out with someone else—whatever works best for you.

AFFIRMATIONS

I am grateful for a place to rest and refill my cup.

ACTIONS

Have lunch out with your colleagues or teammates.

AFFIRMATIONS

I am grateful that my needs are met each day.

ACTIONS

Find a piece of art—music, movie, book, painting, any other medium—that resonates with you and learn about the inspiration or story behind it.

AFFIRMATIONS

I am aligned with the forces of gratitude in the world.

ACTIONS

Visit a nearby park or any outdoor spot where you can sit and watch the world carry on around you. Stay for a bit and make a mental note of all the positive things you observe.

AFFIRMATIONS

I raise my vibrations with gratitude.

ACTIONS

Think about your favourite scent. Write about how it makes you feel or what memories it calls to mind.

AFFIRMATIONS

I express
gratitude loudly
and with pride.

ACTIONS

What's the best piece of advice you've ever received? Pass it along to someone else.

AFFIRMATIONS

Life is good.

ACTIONS

Keep a gratitude journal and take time to list the positive things you experience every day.

AFFIRMATIONS

I hold on to gratitude through both highs and lows.

ACTIONS

Tidy up your favourite spot or treasured personal space at home.

AFFIRMATIONS

I choose to see the best in others.

ACTIONS

List down 5 things you're grateful for in the city you live in.

AFFIRMATIONS

I appreciate every new day as a beautiful gift.

ACTIONS

At places you regularly frequent, learn the servers' or staff's first names and make it a point to use these.

AFFIRMATIONS

I choose gratitude mindfully and with the utmost intention.

ACTIONS

Take a moment to recognise how you are a blessing in others' lives.

AFFIRMATIONS

I am in awe of all the forces of nature.

ACTIONS

Right this very moment, stop and look around you. What's one beautiful, inspiring, or overall positive thing you notice?

AFFIRMATIONS

I am grateful for all the love in my life and every expression of love that comes my way.

ACTIONS

In the coming week, share 3 of your simplest pleasures with others.

AFFIRMATIONS

Gratitude brings me a deep sense of joy and happiness.

ACTIONS

Close your eyes, place your palm on your chest and feel your heartbeat. Take a quiet moment to appreciate what it means to be alive.

AFFIRMATIONS

I am eternally grateful for my very existence.

ACTIONS

Write about something that gives you hope and makes you optimistic about the future.

AFFIRMATIONS

My soul sings
with gratitude.

ACTIONS

Dedicate a social media post to celebrating your spouse or best friend.

AFFIRMATIONS

The more thankful I am, the more content I become.

ACTIONS

Give your boss or client a random token of appreciation.

AFFIRMATIONS

I am grateful to have a job that sustains me.

ACTIONS

Think of a time someone had your back. How might you do the same for someone else?

AFFIRMATIONS

I appreciate all the sources of positivity in my life.

ACTIONS

Thinking of the kids in your life, what can you learn from them and how they see the world?

AFFIRMATIONS

I am always sincere in my expressions of thanks.

ACTIONS

List down 5 things that bring you comfort.

AFFIRMATIONS

I appreciate everything I have exactly for what it is—nothing more, and nothing less.

ACTIONS

Make it a point to eat meals mindfully, really savouring and appreciating the tastes and sensations of your food.

AFFIRMATIONS

I am grateful for the abundance of good that permeates every aspect of my life.

ACTIONS

When faced with 'challenging' individuals and people you don't quite get along the best with, try to list down 3 positive things about them in your head.

AFFIRMATIONS

There is something to be grateful for everywhere I go, and in everything I see.

ACTIONS

Write about your best childhood memory.

AFFIRMATIONS

I choose
to flourish
and grow in
gratitude.

ACTIONS

Ask a close friend or loved one to share one of their favourite memories with you.

Also available by **Kathy Shanks**...

Guided Journaling is available worldwide as print or ebook at Amazon, Booktopia, Barnes & Noble and all good bookstores.

Also available in Australia from **turtlepublishing.com.au**

Inside this book you'll discover how to use my method of journaling to:

- Work towards creating balance for heart, mind, body and soul without sacrificing career and relationships
- Create rituals that help you develop gratitude
- Use daily affirmations to practice positivity and manifest your future dreams
- Discover strategies to improve your relationships, build your life mission, start a side hustle, discover yourself, develop self-love, improve your health AND improve your mindset

It seems too good to be true, right! Organising your thoughts and dreams in 10-20 minutes a day can be that one simple change that actually makes your dreams become a reality.

Make your journal your safe haven, a place of nurturing for you to come and reflect, clear your mind, set goals, develop gratitude, make plans, dream, and take steps towards the future that has always seemed just out of reach.

Please join our journaling community at
facebook.com/groups/kathyshanks
for exclusive insider access to updates and releases

Also available in the
Guided Journaling Series...

Journaling for a
Balanced Life with a
Health focus

Journaling for a
Balanced Life with a
Life Mission focus

Journaling for a
Balanced Life with a
focus on the **Heart**

Journaling for a
Balanced Life with a
Gratitude & **Manifest** focus

We have a selection of *journals* available worldwide as
print or ebook at Amazon, Booktopia,
Barnes & Noble and all good bookstores.
Also available in Australia from **turtlepublishing.com.au**

www.ingramcontent.com/pod-product-compliance
Lightning Source LLC
Chambersburg PA
CBHW020323010526
44107CB00054B/1955